Profiles of the Presidents

JAMES K. POLK

★ ★ ★

Profiles of the Presidents

JAMES K. POLK

by Barbara A. Somervill

Content Advisers: John Holtzapple, Director, and Tom Price, Curator, James K. Polk Ancestral Home, Columbia, Tennessee
Reading Adviser: Dr. Linda D. Labbo, Department of Reading Education, College of Education, The University of Georgia

COMPASS POINT BOOKS ✦ MINNEAPOLIS, MINNESOTA

Compass Point Books
3109 West 50th Street, #115
Minneapolis, MN 55410

Visit Compass Point Books on the Internet at *www.compasspointbooks.com*
or e-mail your request to *custserv@compasspointbooks.com*

Photographs ©: White House Collection, Courtesy White House Historical Association (30), cover, 3;
The Maryland Historical Society, Baltimore, Maryland, 6; National Portrait Gallery, Smithsonian
Institution/Art Resource, N.Y., 7 (top); North Wind Picture Archives, 7 (bottom), 14, 32, 33, 35, 36, 37,
40, 58 (left, all); Library of Congress, 8, 15, 18, 23, 25, 27, 39, 46, 47, 59 (bottom right); Hulton/Archive
by Getty Images, 9, 19 (all), 29, 31, 41, 54 (right, all), 55 (right, all), 57 (top right), 59 (top right);
Michael Evans/The Image Finders, 11, 54 (left); Courtesy of the National Library of Medicine, 12;
Southern Historical Collection, Wilson Library, University of North Carolina at Chapel Hill, 13, 55 (left);
Lombard Antiquarian Maps & Prints, 16, 26, 30, 38; James K. Polk Memorial Association, 17, 50 (top),
56 (left); The North Carolina Collection, University of North Carolina at Chapel Hill Libraries, 20;
Tennessee State Library & Archives, 21, 56 (left); David J. & Janice L. Frent Collection/Corbis, 22;
Stock Montage, 43; Corbis, 44; Tennessee State Museum Collection, photo by June Dorman, 49, 59 (left);
Unicorn Stock Photos/Robin Rudd, 50 (bottom); Department of Rare Books and Special Collections,
University of Rochester Library, 56 (right); Texas State Library & Archives Commission, 57 (bottom right);
Bruce Burkhardt/Corbis, 58 (top right); PhotoDisc, 58 (bottom right).

Editors: E. Russell Primm, Emily J. Dolbear, Melissa McDaniel, and Catherine Neitge
Photo Researcher: Svetlana Zhurkina
Photo Selector: Linda S. Koutris
Designer: The Design Lab
Cartographer: XNR Productions, Inc.

Library of Congress Cataloging-in-Publication Data
Somervill, Barbara A.
  James K. Polk / by Barbara A. Somervill.
    p. cm. — (Profiles of the presidents)
  Summary: A biography of the eleventh president of the United States,
discussing his personal life, education, and political career.
  Includes bibliographical references (p.) and index.
  ISBN 0-7565-0259-4 (hardcover : alk. paper)
  1. Polk, James K. (James Knox), 1795–1849—Juvenile literature. 2. Presidents—United States—
Biography—Juvenile literature. [1. Polk, James K. (James Knox), 1795–1849. 2. Presidents.] I. Title. II.
Series.
  E417 .S66 2003
  973.6'1'092—dc21   2002153305

Printed in the United States of America.

Table of Contents

★   ★   ★

*NOTE: In this book, words that are defined in the glossary are in **bold** the first time they appear in the text.*

The First Dark Horse

★ ★ ★

In 1844, leaders of the Democratic Party gathered in Baltimore, Maryland, to choose their **candidate** for

Odd Fellows Hall in
Baltimore, Maryland

president. It was a struggle. Strong opinions divided party members. People argued on the meeting floor, in private rooms, and in the hallways of Baltimore's Odd Fellows Hall. Many Democrats favored former president Martin Van Buren. Others wanted Lewis Cass, a politician from Michigan.

A new rule made choosing a candidate difficult. The candidate had to win two-thirds of the votes at the meeting. Van

Buren earned just more than half the votes, but he did not come close to getting two-thirds. Southern Democrats did not vote for Van Buren because he was against adding Texas to the United States. Most Southerners wanted Texas to join the Union because, like their states, Texas would allow slavery.

◄ Martin Van Buren was unpopular with Southern Democrats who wanted to see Texas join the Union.

On the eighth vote, Democrats added another name to the **ballot**—James Knox Polk. He had been a member of the U.S. House of Representatives. He had served as Speaker of the House, the top position in that branch of Congress. Polk, however, had left national politics five

◄ Michigan Democrat Lewis Cass also hoped to run for president in 1844.

James K. Polk was the first dark horse candidate to run in a presidential election.

years earlier to return to Tennessee. When the votes were counted on the eighth ballot, Polk came in third behind Van Buren and Cass.

The ninth ballot changed everything. Not only did James K. Polk win, but he received 100 percent of the votes. Many Democrats wondered if Polk had any chance of beating the Whig party candidate, Henry Clay. Compared to Clay, Polk was unknown.

Polk became the first **dark horse** candidate for U.S. president. This term is used in horse racing when an unknown horse beats the one everyone thought would win.

The Whigs laughed when the Democrats chose Polk. They thought Clay had won the election before voters even went to the polls. Clay's **campaign** asked the question, "Who is James K. Polk?"

JUSTICE TO — HARRY OF THE WEST.

GRAND NATIONAL WHIG BANNER.
"ONWARD!"

◀ *A banner from 1844 encouraging voters to elect Whig presidential candidate Henry Clay*

When the votes were finally counted, the Democrats answered the Whigs' question. James K. Polk was the new president of the United States.

The Early Years

★ ★ ★

James Knox Polk was born on November 2, 1795. He was the first child born to Samuel and Jane Knox Polk. They lived in a log house on a 250-acre (618-hectare) farm near Pineville, North Carolina.

Jane Polk came from a deeply religious background and believed in hard work and strict rules. Five more sons and four daughters were born after James. The Polk children helped with chores around the house and farm. James, however, was sickly. He was too weak to work in the fields.

In 1803, Ezekiel Polk, James's grandfather, moved from Pineville onto some land in Tennessee, near present-day Columbia. Tennessee was wild country in the 1800s. Ezekiel started a new farm in this rugged area.

Three years later, Samuel, Jane, and their children joined the older Polks in Tennessee. To get there, the family traveled over 500 miles (805 kilometers) of rutted roads and wagon tracks. When they arrived, they built a new log cabin and cleared their land to plant corn and tobacco. Like many Southern farm families, the Polks relied on slave labor.

By 1812, James's health troubles had grown worse. The local doctor had no idea what was wrong with him. The family decided that he should go to Pennsylvania to see a famous doctor there. To get to Pennsylvania, James lay on thick padding in the back of a wagon driven by his father. The two never made it as far as Pennsylvania.

▼ *The log buildings at the Polk Memorial in Pineville, North Carolina, are furnished as they would have been when Polk was born.*

Dr. Ephraim McDowell successfully operated on the young James Polk in 1812.

By the time they reached Kentucky, James became too sick to travel. In Kentucky, Dr. Ephraim McDowell saw James and said that he needed bladder surgery right away.

McDowell strapped James tightly to a board. Then he started to operate. McDowell gave James no painkillers. He did not clean the wound. He did not do anything to make his surgeon's tools perfectly clean, as doctors do today. Doctors in 1812 did not know how important cleanliness was. Surprisingly, the operation on his bladder was a success. James recovered quickly and returned to Tennessee healthy.

His parents decided James would do better in business than in farming and sent him to school. He entered the Zion Church School at age seventeen, many years older than the other students. After that, he went to the Bradley Academy in nearby Murfreesboro. In less than three years at those two schools, he learned enough to be ready for college.

James decided to return to North Carolina to attend school. At the University of North Carolina in Chapel Hill, he studied mathematics, Latin, and Greek. He enjoyed college life and was an active member of the school's **debate** team. He graduated in 1818 with high honors.

◄ *This unique paper cutout of the University of North Carolina was made in 1818.*

Felix Grundy ▶

After graduation, Polk decided to become a lawyer. He went to Nashville, Tennessee, to study with a well-known attorney named Felix Grundy. During the 1800s, people who wanted to be lawyers studied with other lawyers instead of going to law school. Polk also worked as a clerk in the Tennessee **legislature.** After a year, he became a lawyer and was ready for a career in politics.

Old Hickory and Young Hickory

★ ★ ★

James Polk's father and grandfather both took an active interest in politics. They became friends with General Andrew Jackson, who was a leading Democrat from Tennessee. Jackson and the elder Polks shared a basic belief that government should be run by the people. The Polks introduced Jackson to young James, and the two men began a lifelong friendship.

Andrew Jackson was a national hero. During the War of 1812 (1812–1814), the United States fought Great Britain. Not having heard that

General Andrew Jackson became a good friend to Polk.

Andrew Jackson (right, waving hat) and American troops during the Battle of New Orleans

the war was officially over, both American and British troops continued to fight at the Battle of New Orleans in 1815. Jackson and his troops defeated the British during this conflict. This victory made Jackson famous.

James Polk admired Jackson. He was happy to follow the older man's political lead. Jackson's tough, rugged ways had earned him the nickname Old Hickory, after the hard wood of the hickory tree. Because of his close friendship with Jackson, Polk became known as Young Hickory.

Jackson played an impor-
tant role in many parts of
Polk's life. Polk fell in love
with Sarah Childress, who was
a friend of the Jackson family.
Sarah was perfect for Polk. At
that time, many women
received little education.
However, Sarah was well edu-
cated. She was also interested
in politics. Sarah read a great
deal and was comfortable discussing a variety of topics.

▲ *Sarah Childress Polk in 1828*

Her family was known throughout Tennessee, which was
helpful for Polk's political future. When Polk asked Sarah
to marry him, she joked that she would if he ran for the
Tennessee House of Representatives and won. He did, and
the two married on January 1, 1824.

That year, Polk supported Andrew Jackson in his run
for the presidency. The election was a four-way race. Jackson, Henry Clay, Secretary of State John Quincy Adams,
and Secretary of the Treasury William H. Crawford all
were running.

Jackson won the most votes in the election, but he did not become president. The president is not chosen by a direct vote of the people. Instead, the person who wins the vote in the **electoral college** becomes president. In the electoral college, each state is given a certain number of votes based on its population. Under the U.S. **Constitution,** a person has to win more than half the electoral college votes to win the election. If no one gets more than 50 percent, then a vote in the House of Representatives decides who will be president.

A political cartoon ▾ from 1824 shows the race for the presidency between candidates (from left) John Quincy Adams, William H. Crawford, and Andrew Jackson. Henry Clay (far right) has dropped out of the race and has his hand on his head.

In 1824, none of the candidates earned enough electoral college votes to win, so it was up to the House of Representatives to decide. Henry Clay had come in fourth, so he was out of the running. Many people thought he and Adams had cut a deal, since most of Clay's supporters in the House backed Adams. As a result, Adams became president and appointed Clay secretary of state, the president's leading adviser for dealing with other countries.

◀ *John Quincy Adams*

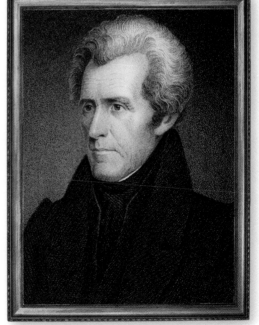

◀ *Andrew Jackson*

The whole affair angered Polk, and as a result, both Jackson and Polk considered Clay an enemy.

In 1825, Polk won a seat in the U.S. House of

Polk moved from ▲
local to national
politics in 1825
when he became
a member of the
U.S. House of
Representatives.

Representatives. He ran as a member of the Democratic-Republican Party, which is today's Democratic Party. Polk served as a representative from 1825 to 1839.

John Quincy Adams served only one term as president. In 1828, Jackson again ran against Adams. This time, Jackson won. Polk became President Jackson's most loyal supporter in Congress.

In general, Polk and Jackson agreed on how the government should run. Polk was against high taxes and tariffs, which are taxes on goods brought into the country. He thought the government should not spend money to build roads, railroads, and bridges. Like Jackson, Polk valued farming and disliked wealthy men who tried to control the government with their money.

From 1835 to 1839, Polk served as Speaker of the House. Having the top job in the House of Representatives was both a blessing and a burden. A new political group called the Whigs had become popular. As Speaker of the House, Polk presented many ideas that the Whigs criticized. By the time Polk's term ended in 1839, he had enough of Washington. He returned to Nashville to run for governor of Tennessee.

Polk served only one two-year term as governor. In 1841, he ran for a second term and lost. Polk left politics and returned to his law practice in Columbia.

▲ *Polk during his term as Speaker of the House*

However, the Democrats did not forget about Polk. When they could not agree on a presidential candidate in 1844, they thought of him. They decided to give the dark horse a chance.

An 1844 campaign ribbon for James K. Polk

Manifest Destiny

★   ★   ★

The 1844 election focused on expanding the United States. One of the most important issues was whether Texas should be added to the Union. It was hard to tell where the Whigs' presidential candidate, Henry Clay, stood on any issue. In one letter published in a newspaper, Clay spoke out against adding Texas to the Union. A few months later, Clay favored it. His opinions seemed to shift to match public views. The Democrats accused Clay of "talking out of both sides of his mouth."

James Polk strongly believed in Manifest Destiny—the idea that the United States had a right to all land

▼ Henry Clay was the Whig candidate for president in 1844.

between the Atlantic and Pacific Oceans. He wanted Texas added to the Union right away.

For most Americans, the argument over Texas was an argument over slavery. Southerners wanted Texas to become a state because it would allow slavery. Texas would increase the power of slave holding states in the federal government. Northerners were against Texas joining the Union because they did not want the South to have more power.

The fate of Oregon was another important issue in the election. In 1844, Oregon Territory included present-day Oregon, Washington, Idaho, and western Canada. The 42nd **parallel** marked the territory's southern border. Polk wanted Oregon's northern border to reach 54° 40' north latitude. However, the British claimed the same territory, and they did not want to give it up.

During the election, Polk used the phrase "Fifty-four Forty or Fight" as his campaign **slogan.** This was a threat to Great Britain to give up its claims to Oregon or be prepared to go to war. In truth, Polk knew that the border would end up being set at the 49th parallel. He also knew that favoring an increase in territory would win him votes.

When the election came, Polk won 1,337,243 votes. Clay received 1,299,062. Another candidate, James Birney, who wanted to outlaw slavery everywhere in the United States, received only 62,300 votes. Birney all but gave Polk the presidency. If Birney had not run, most of the votes cast for him would likely have gone to Clay. In New York alone, Birney's votes changed the results for the entire nation. Had Clay earned 5,000 more votes in New York, he would have won the state's electoral votes and the presidency. As it was, James K. Polk won with 49.5 percent of the vote.

◄ James G. Birney ran for president in 1844. Although he lost, Birney took away anough votes from Clay to help Polk win the election.

*Sarah Polk ▸
had strong
religious opinions.*

Just before Polk took office, President John Tyler asked
Congress to add Texas to the United States. Congress
agreed. Eventually, Texas would become the twenty-eighth
state in the Union.

James and Sarah Polk moved into the White House in
March 1845. Sarah Polk was a religious Presbyterian. She

refused to allow dancing or card playing in the White House. Because the Polks had no children, Sarah devoted her time to helping her husband with his work. She often read newspapers for James, and she told him her opinions about politics and government.

Shortly after taking office, Polk received a letter from Jackson. His old friend was dying. That night, Polk wrote in his diary, "Received today . . . a letter from Andrew Jackson written on the 6th June . . . two days before his death, and the last letter he ever wrote. . . .

▼ *Andrew Jackson on his deathbed in June 1845*

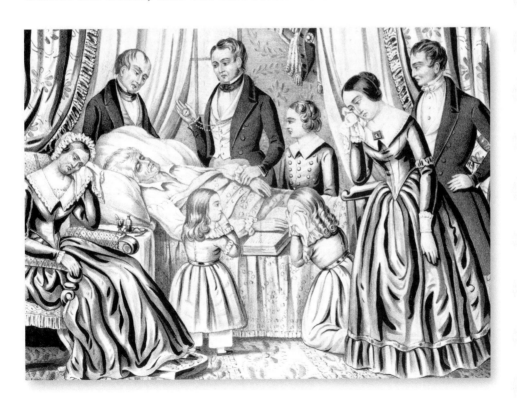

It will be preserved as a highly prized memorial of the friendship of the dying patriot, a friendship which had never for a moment been broken from my early youth until the day of his death."

James Polk set four main goals for himself as president: He wanted to settle the Oregon question with Great Britain quickly. He hoped to add California to the United States and planned to reduce tariffs. Finally, he wanted to set up a treasury department that was free from outside pressures.

Polk had his hands full from the start of his presidency. Events in Texas heated up almost immediately. Mexico and

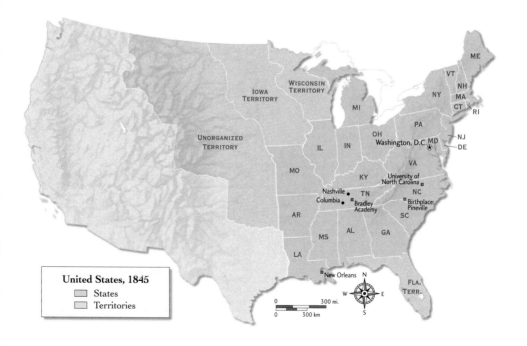

United States, 1845
— States
— Territories

the United States disagreed about the location of the
Texas-Mexico border. What was worse, Mexico did not
agree that Texas was a separate country that was free to
join the United States. Mexico also demanded that
Americans leave present-day California, which at the
time was Mexican territory. It seemed that Mexico and
the United States would go to war.

In June 1845, Polk sent General Zachary Taylor
and his troops to protect Americans living in southern

▼ *Austin, Texas, in
the 1840s*

Texas. The troops were ordered to remain north of the Rio Grande. Polk had chosen John Slidell, a congressman from Louisiana, to be the American **minister** to Mexico. He sent Slidell to Mexico City to discuss buying California.

The Mexicans sent Slidell home. They demanded that Taylor's troops move north from the Rio Grande

General Zachary Taylor (second from left) and his troops were assigned the task of protecting Americans living in southern Texas.

◄ *John Slidell tried to buy California from Mexico, but Mexico would not sell it.*

to the Rio Nueces. The Mexican army then moved north of the Rio Grande. They attacked a small group of American soldiers in April 1846, killing eleven of them. Polk told Congress, "Mexico has invaded our territory and shed American blood upon the American soil." On May 13, the United States declared war against Mexico.

Oregon Territory in the 1850s ▲

Polk had to handle more than just the Texas situation, however. He wanted to make sure Oregon would be part of the United States, so that slave and non-slave regions would be balanced. Great Britain and the United States had "shared" Oregon since 1818. Now, Polk wanted the United States to have sole claim to the region. He pushed to have Oregon's northern border set at 54° 40' north latitude. In June, however, Polk finally accepted Great Britain's offer of a border set at the 49th parallel. He had no time to talk about it anymore—he was too busy addressing the war with Mexico.

The Hardest Working President

★   ★   ★

The president is officially the commander in chief of the U.S. Army. Polk took this role to heart. He planned battles, decided where to send troops, and even bought mules for carrying army supplies. However, the Mexican War (1846–1848) still got off to a poor start.

Congress had little interest in the war. Generals Zachary Taylor and Winfield Scott, who were in charge of fighting the war, did not seem

▾ *General Winfield Scott*

to care either. They seemed more concerned about their own popularity than winning battles. Polk said: "I am in the unenviable position of being held responsible for the conduct of the Mexican War, when I have no support either from Congress or from the two officers highest in command in the field."

In fairness to Scott and Taylor, the chances of winning the war did not look good. American soldiers were not used to the hot, humid Mexican summer. To make matters worse, they wore warm wool uniforms. Some soldiers passed out from the heat.

Soon, more than one hundred thousand U.S. soldiers were fighting the war. They had to be supplied with guns, bullets, food, and clothing. As the army moved into Mexico, getting supplies to the troops became nearly impossible. Supplies got bogged down in swamps, herds of mules ran away, and Mexican soldiers attacked supply troops. American soldiers became sick with serious diseases. Many died before the first battle was ever fought.

The Mexican War was also fought in California. Some of the officers there had only recently graduated from West Point, the U.S. military academy. These young officers quickly took over San Francisco, Sacramento, and

Monterey, California. This made Polk even more annoyed at Taylor and Scott as they moved slowly through Mexico. He would have gladly traded his two generals for a handful of gritty West Point captains. He said, "The truth is that the old army officers have become so in the

▼ *U.S. troops landing at the Mexican coastal town of Veracruz during the Mexican War*

Cadets at West ▶
Point in the 1850s;
Polk admired
the energetic
young soldiers.

habit of enjoying their ease, sitting in parlors and on carpeted floors, that most of them have no energy."

Congress had to pass a special bill, or proposed law, to pay for the Mexican War. Pennsylvania representative David Wilmot added an extra section to the bill, called the Wilmot Proviso. This section said that slavery would not be allowed in any territory gained from Mexico during the war.

The Wilmot Proviso split the political parties in half. Democrats and Whigs from the North voted for the bill. Democrats and Whigs from the South voted against it. The bill failed in the Senate, and money to fight the war became tied up by political arguments.

◄ *Pennsylvania representative David Wilmot*

As the war dragged on, Polk came up with a bold plan to end it. In July 1846, Polk decided to enlist the help of General Santa Anna, the former head of the

General Santa Anna ▼

Mexican army. Ten years earlier, Santa Anna had led the Mexican army against Texans at the Battle of the Alamo. At that time, Texas was part of Mexico, and the Texans were trying to make it an independent country. Many Texans died at the Alamo, and people in that state still hated Santa Anna. However, Polk's solution to the Mexican War was to allow Santa Anna to return to Mexico. In return, Santa Anna was expected to arrange peace between Mexico and the United States.

The plan turned out to be almost unbelievably disastrous. When Santa Anna arrived in Mexico City, he did not help make peace. Instead, he was named leader of the Mexican army. He rebuilt the army and headed north to attack Zachary Taylor's troops at Monterrey, Mexico. Although Taylor had only 6,000 men, they defeated Santa Anna's 18,000 soldiers. Taylor became a hero, while Polk gritted his teeth in embarrassment.

Meanwhile, the war continued in the West. Polk still had a government to run. He worked long hours

▲ *The Battle of Monterrey was a victory for General Taylor's troops.*

The building that ▸
housed the U.S.
Treasury Department
in Washingon,
D.C., in 1850

every day, and the work paid off. In 1846, Polk achieved
two of the main goals of his presidency.

One of these goals was to set up a treasury department. Polk's Independent Treasury Act of 1846 estab-
lished a department to manage government money. The
U.S. Treasury Department that exists today began with
this act in 1846.

That same year, Polk followed through on his goal
of lowering tariffs. By taxing goods brought into this

country, tariffs make foreign products more expensive. This in turn helps American businesses because people are more likely to buy the less expensive American goods.

▼ Foreign goods arriving in the U.S. on ships like this one would have been more expensive during the 1850s because of tariffs.

Many Northerners wanted high tariffs so Northern businesses would have an easier time competing against European companies. Many Southerners bought European products such as cloth, metal goods, and furniture. They wanted lower tariffs so these products would be less expensive. The new lower tariff was also popular in the West.

With the banking and tariff issues settled, Polk turned his attention once more to Mexico. In 1847, General Winfield Scott finally came up with a battle plan. He set out from Veracruz, Mexico, toward the capital, Mexico City. Scott's men were outnumbered and cut off from supplies, yet they moved on. When they reached the capital, they engaged in hand-to-hand fighting against the Mexicans. Scott captured Mexico City in September 1847.

The United States was now firmly in control of the war. Polk decided to force Mexico to sign a treaty, or agreement, ending it. The Mexican War officially ended with the Treaty of Guadalupe Hidalgo. This agreement set the Texas-Mexico border at the Rio Grande. As part of the treaty, Mexico also agreed to sell California, Arizona, New Mexico, and parts of Nevada, Colorado, and Utah

General Winfield
Scott as he
entered
Mexico City in
September 1847

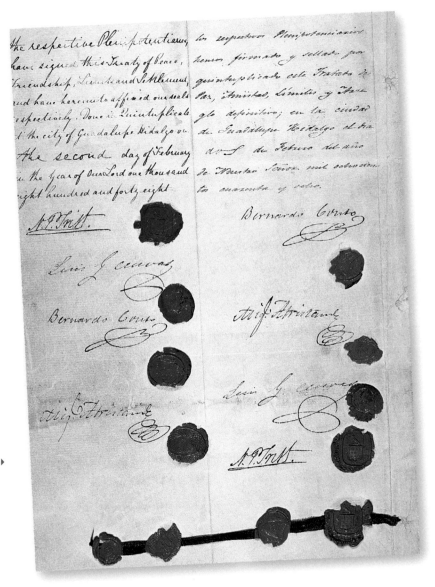

A page from the ▶
Treaty of Guadalupe
Hidalgo, which ended
the Mexican War and
gave new territory to
the United States

to the United States for just $15 million. During Polk's presidency, the United States acquired more than 1 million square miles (2.6 million square kilometers) of land.

The End of the Road

★ ★ ★

Polk found being president a terrible burden. He claimed, "With me, it is . . . true that the presidency is 'no bed of roses.'"

Polk was one of the most successful presidents in history. He achieved all of his major goals in only four years. By the end of his term, the United States had grown and stretched from the Atlantic to the Pacific. The land added to the country during Polk's presidency eventually became the states of Washington, Oregon, Idaho, California, Nevada, Arizona, New Mexico, Utah, and Colorado.

When Polk became president, he swore that he would serve only one term. He kept his promise. He had never enjoyed good health, and the presidency had left him exhausted.

The 1848 election would decide who would follow Polk as president. During this election, General Zachary

ZACHARY TAYLOR,
PEOPLE'S CANDIDATE FOR PRESIDENT.

MILLARD FILLMORE,
WHIG CANDIDATE FOR VICE PRESIDENT.

An 1848 campaign ▲ poster for Whig presidential candidate Zachary Taylor and his running mate, Millard Fillmore

Taylor ran against Lewis Cass of Michigan and former president Martin Van Buren. Polk had disliked Taylor from the start of the Mexican War. Taylor, he said, "is evidently a weak man and has been made giddy with the idea of the Presidency. . . . He is a narrow-minded, bigoted person."

To Polk's dismay, General Zachary Taylor was elected the twelfth president. Polk wrote in his diary, "The election of General Taylor as President . . . is deeply to be regretted. . . . He is wholly unqualified for the station."

Taylor was sworn in as president in March 1849. James Polk, leaving office, said, "I feel exceedingly relieved that I am free from all public cares." James and Sarah Polk left Washington. They planned a long, comfortable retirement in Nashville, Tennessee.

▼ *Taylor delivers his first speech as the new president of the United States.*

Instead of returning directly to Tennessee, the Polks decided to tour the Southern states. Along the way, Polk made many speeches to the public. Within two weeks, Polk's health suffered from the strains of travel.

He grew weaker, and he stopped eating because of terrible stomach pains. The trip dragged on. The Polks were forced to often stop along the way to allow him to rest.

The rest did not help. In June, Polk again fell ill with stomach pains. This time, he had a serious disease

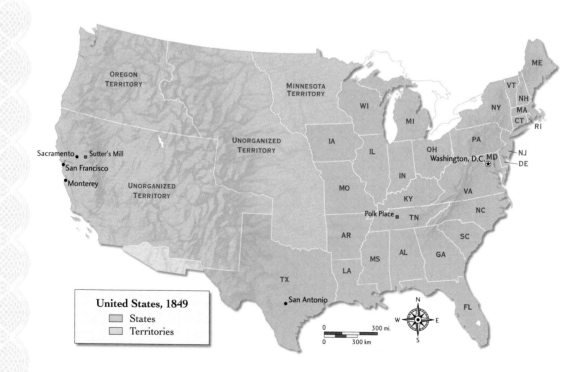

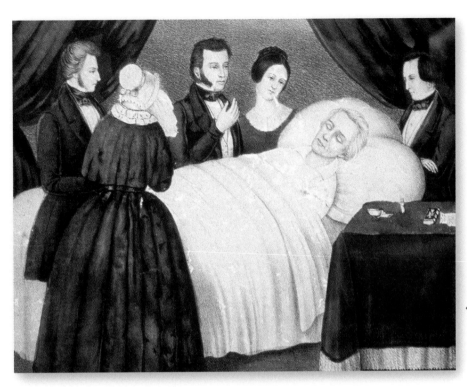

◀ *Polk on his deathbed in June 1849*

called cholera. Polk died on June 15, 1849. He was buried at his home in Nashville.

On his deathbed, Polk asked Sarah to free their slaves when she died. Sarah lived forty-two more years. The Civil War (1861–1865) freed their slaves long before her death.

Polk remains one of the least known, yet most effective, presidents in U.S. history. He was one of the few presidents to achieve most of his goals. His main failure may have been not realizing how deeply slavery divided

the North from the South. Polk's destiny was to help the country achieve its own Manifest Destiny. In this—above all else—he succeeded.

Sarah Polk lived forty-two more years after her husband died.

The tomb of James and Sarah Polk on the grounds of the state capitol in Nashville

GLOSSARY

★ ★ ★

ballot—a vote

campaign—an organized effort to win an election

candidate—someone running for office in an election

Constitution—the document stating the basic laws of the United States

dark horse—a candidate who is not well known

debate—a formal argument

electoral college—a group of people who elect the U.S. president; each state is given a certain number of electoral votes; the candidate who receives the most votes from the people is awarded the state's electoral votes

legislature—the part of government that makes or changes laws

minister—an official who represents one country in another country

parallel—a line of latitude around Earth, marking the distance from the equator

slogan—a phrase used to capture public attention in a campaign

JAMES K. POLK'S LIFE AT A GLANCE

★ ★ ★

PERSONAL

Nickname:	Young Hickory
Birth date:	November 2, 1795
Birthplace:	Near Pineville, North Carolina
Father's name:	Samuel Polk
Mother's name:	Jane Knox Polk
Education:	Graduated from the University of North Carolina in 1818
Wife's name:	Sarah Childress Polk (1803–1891)
Married:	January 1, 1824
Children:	None
Died:	June 15, 1849, in Nashville, Tennessee
Buried:	Nashville, Tennessee

PUBLIC

Occupation before presidency:	Lawyer, public official
Occupation after presidency:	None
Military service:	None
Other government positions:	Member of the Tennessee House of Representatives; member of the U.S. House of Representatives; governor of Tennessee
Political party:	Democrat
Vice president:	George M. Dallas (1845–1849)
Dates in office:	March 4, 1845–March 3, 1849
Presidential opponent:	Henry Clay (Whig), 1844
Number of votes (Electoral College):	1,338,464 of 2,638,305 (170 of 275), 1844
Writings:	*The Diary of James K. Polk* (4 volumes) (1910)

★

James K. Polk's Cabinet

Secretary of state:
  James Buchanan (1845–1849)

Secretary of the treasury:
  Robert J. Walker (1845–1849)

Secretary of war:
  William L. Marcy (1845–1849*

Attorney general:
  John Y. Mason (1845–1846)
  Nathan Clifford (1846–1848)
  Isaac Toucey (1848–1849)

Postmaster general:
  Cave Johnson (1845–1849)

Secretary of the navy:
  George Bancroft (1845–1846)
  John Y. Mason (1846–1849)

JAMES K. POLK'S LIFE AND TIMES

★ ★ ★

POLK'S LIFE

WORLD EVENTS

1791   Austrian composer Wolfgang Amadeus Mozart (below) dies

November 2, James Knox Polk is born near Pineville, North Carolina (below)   1795

1799   Napoléon Bonaparte (right) takes control of France

1800

1801   Ultraviolet radiation is discovered

POLK'S LIFE		WORLD EVENTS

POLK'S LIFE

The Polk family moves to Tennessee 1806

WORLD EVENTS

1807 Robert Fulton's *Clermont* (right) is the first reliable steamship to travel between New York City and Albany

1809 American poet and short-story writer Edgar Allen Poe is born in Boston

1810 1810 Bernardo O'Higgins leads Chile in its fight for independence from Spain

1812-1814 The United States and Britain fight the War of 1812 (right)

1814-1815 European states meet in Vienna, Austria, to redraw national borders after the conclusion of the Napoleonic Wars

Graduates with high honors from the University of North Carolina (above) 1818

POLK'S LIFE

Becomes a lawyer   1820

Wins election to the   1823
Tennessee legislature

Marries Sarah   1824
Childress (below)

Elected to the U.S.   1825
House of
Representatives

1820

WORLD EVENTS

1820   Susan B. Anthony
(right), a leader
of the
American
woman
suffrage
movement,
is born

1823   Mexico becomes
a republic

1826   The first photograph
is taken by Joseph
Niépce, a French
physicist

1827   Modern-day matches
are invented by
coating the end of a
wooden stick with
phosphorus

★

POLK'S LIFE

WORLD EVENTS

1830

1829   The first practical sewing machine is invented by French tailor Barthélemy Thimonnier (right)

1833   Great Britain abolishes slavery

Becomes Speaker of the House of Representatives   1835

1836   Texans defeat Mexican troops at San Jacinto after a deadly battle at the Alamo (below)

1837   American banker J. P. Morgan is born

Becomes governor of Tennessee   1839

★

POLK'S LIFE

WORLD EVENTS

1840

1840   Auguste Rodin, famous sculptor of *The Thinker* (right), is born

Presidential Election Results:	Popular Votes	Electoral Votes
1844 James K. Polk	1,338,464	170
Henry Clay	1,300,097	105

Texas becomes the twenty-eighth state   1845

The Mexican War begins   1846

Polk settles dispute with Great Britain over the Oregon Territory (left)

Signs a bill lowering tariffs

Signs a bill establishing the U.S. Treasury Department (below)

1846   Irish potato famine reaches its worst

German astronomer Johann Gottfried Galle discovers Neptune (below)

POLK'S LIFE

WORLD EVENTS

Signs the Treaty
of Guadalupe
Hidalgo ending the
Mexican War

1848

1848

*The Communist
Manifesto,* by German
writer Karl Marx
(below), is widely
distributed

June 15, dies from
cholera at his home
in Tennessee

1849

1850

1852

American Harriet
Beecher Stowe (below)
publishes *Uncle
Tom's Cabin*

UNDERSTANDING JAMES K. POLK AND HIS PRESIDENCY

★ ★ ★

IN THE LIBRARY

Gaines, Ann Graham. *James Polk: Our Eleventh President.*
Chanhassen, Minn.: The Child's World, 2002.

Lindop, Edmund. *James Polk, Abraham Lincoln, Theodore Roosevelt.*
Brookfield, Conn.: Twenty-first Century Books, 1997.

Tibbitts, Alison Davis. *James K. Polk: Manifest Destiny.*
Springfield, N.J.: Enslow Publishers, 1999.

ON THE WEB

Internet Public Library—James K. Polk
http://www.ipl.org/ref/POTUS/jkpolk.html
For information about Polk's presidency
and many links to other resources

The American President—James K. Polk
http://www.americanpresident.org/history/jamespolk/
For an in-depth look at Polk's life and career

The White House—James K. Polk
http://www.whitehouse.gov/history/presidents/jp11.html
For a short biography of Polk

POLK HISTORIC SITES
ACROSS THE COUNTRY

James K. Polk Gravesite
Tennessee State Capitol
Charlotte Avenue
Nashville, TN 37243
To visit Polk's grave

James K. Polk Ancestral Home
301 West Seventh Street
Columbia, TN 38401
931/388-2354
To visit the house where Polk lived as a young man

Polk's Birthplace
James K. Polk Memorial
308 S. Polk Street
Pineville, NC 28134
704/889-7145
To see rough log cabins furnished
as they would have been when Polk was born

THE U.S. PRESIDENTS
(Years in Office)

★ ★ ★

1. **George Washington**
(March 4, 1789-March 3, 1797)
2. **John Adams**
(March 4, 1797-March 3, 1801)
3. **Thomas Jefferson**
(March 4, 1801-March 3, 1809)
4. **James Madison**
(March 4, 1809-March 3, 1817)
5. **James Monroe**
(March 4, 1817-March 3, 1825)
6. **John Quincy Adams**
(March 4, 1825-March 3, 1829)
7. **Andrew Jackson**
(March 4, 1829-March 3, 1837)
8. **Martin Van Buren**
(March 4, 1837-March 3, 1841)
9. **William Henry Harrison**
(March 6, 1841-April 4, 1841)
10. **John Tyler**
(April 6, 1841-March 3, 1845)
11. James K. Polk
(March 4, 1845-March 3, 1849)
12. **Zachary Taylor**
(March 5, 1849-July 9, 1850)
13. **Millard Fillmore**
(July 10, 1850-March 3, 1853)
14. **Franklin Pierce**
(March 4, 1853-March 3, 1857)
15. **James Buchanan**
(March 4, 1857-March 3, 1861)
16. **Abraham Lincoln**
(March 4, 1861-April 15, 1865)
17. **Andrew Johnson**
(April 15, 1865-March 3, 1869)

18. **Ulysses S. Grant**
(March 4, 1869-March 3, 1877)
19. **Rutherford B. Hayes**
(March 4, 1877-March 3, 1881)
20. **James Garfield**
(March 4, 1881-Sept 19, 1881)
21. **Chester Arthur**
(Sept 20, 1881-March 3, 1885)
22. **Grover Cleveland**
(March 4, 1885-March 3, 1889)
23. **Benjamin Harrison**
(March 4, 1889-March 3, 1893)
24. **Grover Cleveland**
(March 4, 1893-March 3, 1897)
25. **William McKinley**
(March 4, 1897-
September 14, 1901)
26. **Theodore Roosevelt**
(September 14, 1901-
March 3, 1909)
27. **William Howard Taft**
(March 4, 1909-March 3, 1913)
28. **Woodrow Wilson**
(March 4, 1913-March 3, 1921)
29. **Warren G. Harding**
(March 4, 1921-August 2, 1923)
30. **Calvin Coolidge**
(August 3, 1923-March 3, 1929)
31. **Herbert Hoover**
(March 4, 1929-March 3, 1933)
32. **Franklin D. Roosevelt**
(March 4, 1933-April 12, 1945)

33. **Harry S. Truman**
(April 12, 1945-
January 20, 1953)
34. **Dwight D. Eisenhower**
(January 20, 1953-
January 20, 1961)
35. **John F. Kennedy**
(January 20, 1961-
November 22, 1963)
36. **Lyndon B. Johnson**
(November 22, 1963-
January 20, 1969)
37. **Richard M. Nixon**
(January 20, 1969-
August 9, 1974)
38. **Gerald R. Ford**
(August 9, 1974-
January 20, 1977)
39. **James Earl Carter**
(January 20, 1977-
January 20, 1981)
40. **Ronald Reagan**
(January 20, 1981-
January 20, 1989)
41. **George H. W. Bush**
(January 20, 1989-
January 20, 1993)
42. **William Jefferson Clinton**
(January 20, 1993-
January 20, 2001)
43. **George W. Bush**
(January 20, 2001-)

INDEX

★ ★ ★

ABOUT THE AUTHOR

Barbara Somervill loves learning. She sees every writing project as a chance to learn new information or gain an understanding of a historic period. Barbara grew up in New York. She has also lived in Toronto, Canada; Canberra, Australia; California; and South Carolina. She is an avid reader and traveler, and enjoys movies and live theater.